# Marvel Studios' Captain America: The First Avenger

Based on the Screenplay by
Christopher Markus and Stephen McFeely
Story by Joe Simon and Jack Kirby

Produced by Kevin Feige, p.g.a.
Directed by Joe Johnston

### Level 2

Retold by Jane Rollason

Series Editors: Andy Hopkins and Jocelyn Potter

T0386041

**Pearson Education Limited**
KAO Two
KAO Park, Harlow,
Essex, CM17 9NA, England
and Associated Companies throughout the world.

ISBN: 978-1-2923-4746-2
This edition first published by Pearson Education Ltd 2018
1 3 5 7 9 10 8 6 4 2

Set in 9pt/14pt Xenois Slab Pro
Printed by Neografia, Slovakia

Published by Pearson Education Limited

For a complete list of the titles available in the Pearson English Readers series, visit
**www.pearsonenglishreaders.com.**
Alternatively, write to your local Pearson Education office or
to Pearson English Readers Marketing Department,
Pearson Education, KAO Two, KAO Park, Harlow, Essex, CM17 9NA

MIX
Paper from
responsible sources
FSC™ C128612

# Contents

# Who's Who?

### Steve Rogers / Captain America

Steve Rogers is a young man from Brooklyn, New York City. His father was a soldier, in the 107th Infantry*, in World War I. His mother worked in a hospital. They are dead, and Steve has no family now.

### James Buchanan "Bucky" Barnes

Bucky Barnes is Steve's best friend from Brooklyn. Bucky was always taller and stronger and often helped his weaker friend. He is now a soldier in the 107th Infantry of the U.S. Army. He is going to fight in Europe.

### Colonel Chester Phillips

Colonel Phillips, a very important soldier, is the head of the S.S.R. (the Strategic Scientific Reserve). This U.S. agency is building guns, bombs—and Super Soldiers—for the fight with the Nazis** and with Hydra, the Nazi science team.

### Agent Peggy Carter

Peggy Carter is British. After her brother died in World War II, she stopped doing desk work for the army. He wanted her to be a British agent, so she worked for the agency MI5. Now she works with the S.S.R.

\* Infantry: foot soldiers, in an army
\*\* Nazis: followers of Adolf Hitler (1889–1945) and his ideas. Many countries fought in World War II (1939–1945) after Hitler's German soldiers went into Poland.

## Howard Stark

Howard Stark is a very rich American with very smart ideas. He is a scientist and he has a big company, Stark Industries. He builds new bombs and guns for the U.S. Army, but he isn't a soldier.

## Dr. Abraham Erskine

Dr. Erskine was born in Germany and worked there on his Super Soldier Serum. When the Nazis started the war in Europe, he moved to the United States. Now he lives in New York City, and he works with the S.S.R.

## Johann Schmidt

Johann Schmidt is a German scientist. Before World War II, he worked with Dr. Erskine on the Super Soldier Serum. He took some of Dr. Erskine's serum and now he is very strong. He is the head of Hydra.

## Dr. Arnim Zola

Dr. Zola is a Nazi scientist. He was born in Switzerland, but now he works for Hydra and Johann Schmidt. He is making very dangerous new bombs for Hydra.

## Hydra

Hydra is a very old and very dangerous organization. The people of Hydra love war. When this story starts, Hydra scientists are making new bombs and guns for the Nazis.

# Introduction

*"With the serum, you will be a very strong man," said Dr. Erskine. "But there is something more important. You are a good man, Steve. With the serum, you will be a great man."*

Steve Rogers is short and weak, and the United States Army doesn't want him. Bullies punch him and girls aren't interested in him. Then, an army scientist gives Steve a super serum. Now, he is super strong. But there is one other man with the serum—Red Skull. He is a very bad man with very dangerous plans for the United States and the world. Can Steve stop Red Skull? Can he save his country and the world?

*Marvel Studios' Captain America: The First Avenger* (2011) is the fifth movie in the Marvel Cinematic Universe. Chris Evans is super strong Steve Rogers. There are two more Captain America movies, and you can also see Captain America in four Avengers films.

The story begins in the middle of World War II (1939–1945). Armies from many countries fought in this war between the "Axis Powers" (Germany, Japan, and Italy) and the "Allied Powers" (the United Kingdom, the United States, China, and Russia). It was a very long and hard war, and many people died. More than 20,000,000 soldiers from all countries died in the war. The United States came into the war after hundreds of Japanese bombs fell on Pearl Harbor, Hawaii, in 1941. After Pearl Harbor, Americans fought in Europe and the Pacific, and 400,000 died.

# Prologue: Norway, 1942

"It's here. I can feel it!"

Johann Schmidt was in a church in a small town in Norway. An old man looked after the church. Schmidt's men watched him, with guns in their hands. Schmidt looked carefully around the church. On one wall, there was a picture of an animal under a tree. Schmidt felt the picture with his fingers. He pushed the eye of the animal.

Suddenly, a door opened in the picture. Schmidt smiled and carefully took out a box. When he opened the box, a strong, blue light shone on his face. He closed it quickly.

"The Tesseract," he said quietly.

"No!" shouted the old man. "It is not for the eyes of men."

"You are right," answered Schmidt, and smiled.

He closed the box and walked out of the church with it.

At the door, he turned and looked at the old man.

"Kill him," he said to his men.

**"The Tesseract," he said quietly.**

# The Boy from Brooklyn

*POW!* Steve fell to the ground. He stood up. *POW!* The man punched him again. The man was taller and heavier than Steve. His hands were as big as Steve's head, but Steve was a brave young man. He stood up again.

"Why don't you walk away?" said the big man.

"I can do this all day!" Steve answered.

The man pulled back his arm, ready for another punch. But suddenly, somebody caught his arm. It was a tall soldier. The soldier pushed the man away from Steve.

"Get out of here," he said. He kicked him, then pushed him out of the street behind the movie theater.

"Bucky!" said Steve, with a smile. "You saved him."

"*Him!*" laughed Bucky. He often had to save his best friend. "What was the fight about this time?"

"We were in the movie theater," Steve told him. "Before the movie, we saw pictures of the war in Europe. American soldiers are dying there, and everybody in the theater watched quietly. But *that* man shouted loudly, 'Why are we watching this? Show us the movie!'"

"Forget him," said Bucky. "I'm going to Europe tomorrow."

"And I'm not," Steve said sadly.

Bucky felt bad. "Let's go dancing, Steve! My ship is leaving in twelve hours."

It was 1943, and the United States was at war. The *world* was at war.

Bucky *and* Steve wanted to fight in the U.S. Army. The army took Bucky—a tall, strong man—and put him in the 107th Infantry. The army didn't want Steve because he was small and weak. He tried for the army in different towns, but the answer was always no.

That week, there was a big show in New York City. It was full of wonderful new ideas for life in the future.

"Let's enjoy my last night at the show," Bucky said to Steve.

When they arrived, there were soldiers everywhere. "Look!" cried Bucky. "Everybody's having a good time. Let's meet some girls." Girls loved Bucky!

"Come and see the car of the future," a man shouted. A lot of people stood around a big, red car. Steve and Bucky stopped and watched. Steve knew the man's face because he was often in the newspapers. His name was Howard Stark, and he was very rich. He was also very smart, and he had many ideas for new things.

"In five years' time, your car ... will fly!" Stark pulled a lever. Slowly, the car started to move up, off the ground ...

"*OOH!*" people shouted. "*AAH!*"

... and then, *BANG!* It fell down again.

"I said 'the car of *tomorrow*'!" laughed Stark. "Not 'the car of *today*'!"

Everybody laughed with him. Bucky talked to some girls, and Steve

looked around. The army was at the show. They always wanted more men, and there were a lot of men here.

*I'll try one more time,* thought Steve. He was smart and he was brave. He could do *something* in this war.

You had to take tests for the army. Bucky found Steve in the test room.

"You're not trying *again*!" said Bucky angrily. "What is this now—the sixth time? They don't want you, Steve. You're too small. Stay at home, and do war work here."

"I *have* to try again," Steve told him. "I have to help my country."

"O.K., Steve," Bucky said. He put out his hand, and Steve took it. This was goodbye. "Be careful."

"Always!" Steve laughed.

Bucky smiled, and left with the girls.

An army doctor came in.

"I heard your conversation with your friend," he said. "You want to go to Europe and fight?"

The doctor was small, with round glasses, and his English was strange. Was this a test?

"Yes, sir," said Steve. Then, he asked, "Excuse me, sir, but where are you from?"

"Queens," said the man, "here in New York City. And before that, Germany. Is that a problem for you?"

"Er ... no," said Steve. "Of course, it isn't." *A German in the U.S. Army*

"I *have* to try again," Steve told him. "I have to help my country."

*is a little strange*, Steve thought. But a lot of Germans lived in New York, and they weren't Nazis.

"I'm Dr. Erskine, from the S.S.R.," the man said. "That's the science agency of the U.S. Army."

"Steve Rogers, sir," said Steve.

Dr. Erskine looked at the papers in front of him. "You had tests in New Haven, in Newark ... five tests in five different cities. Where are you *really* from, Mr. Rogers?"

"Here, sir," Steve told him. "I'm a boy from Brooklyn."

"So, Mr. Rogers," said Dr. Erskine, "this is your sixth test. You really want to be a soldier! I like that."

"Yes, sir," he answered.

"So, do you want to kill some Nazis?"

"I don't *want* to kill anybody. But I don't like bullies."

Dr. Erskine smiled. He really liked Steve.

"I have an interesting job for somebody," he said. "You can try for it. Other men will try, too. Maybe you will get the job, and maybe you won't. I will see you at the Lehigh army base in one week's time."

Steve was very excited. "I'm going to be a soldier!" he shouted.

## "Is This a Test?"

There was a Nazi base high in the mountains, and only a small number of people knew about it. Scientists worked there on ideas for better guns and bombs for Hitler's army. The head of the base was Johann Schmidt, and his top scientist was Dr. Zola. The two men were in a large room with glass windows. Through the windows, they could see only sky and snow.

In the center of the room, there was a strange machine, with smaller machines all around it. Schmidt took the Tesseract out of its box, and put it carefully into the machine.

Dr. Zola quickly put on dark glasses because the blue light was too strong for his eyes. He pushed a lever on the machine.

"Twenty ... thirty ... forty ...," he said.

Schmidt moved Dr. Zola out of the way.

"Let's be brave, Dr. Zola!" He pushed the lever to the top. "One hundred!"

*BUZZZZ! BUZZZZ!* Blue light ran everywhere, around the room. *BANG!* Machines jumped into life. *FLASH!* Lights went on and off. Schmidt and Dr. Zola watched with wide eyes. And then everything went quiet.

"The Tesseract will power my new ideas!" Dr. Zola said slowly. "It will change the war!"

"You're wrong, Dr. Zola," answered Schmidt. "It will change the *world!*"

A week after the show in New York City, Steve stood in line with eleven other soldiers. They were all tall and strong. Steve always felt small, but next to these men, he felt *very* small.

They were at the Lehigh army base in Virginia. Two men and a woman stood in front of them. One of the men was Colonel Phillips. He had lines on his face, and intelligent brown eyes. This man knew all about war.

"Listen, men," he said. "We have the best people in the S.S.R. I have two of them here. You know Dr. Erskine. And this is Agent Carter, from the British Army."

The men looked at Peggy Carter.

"Nice legs," said one soldier quietly.

"Pretty face," laughed the man next to him.

"Isn't this the *U.S.* Army?" the first soldier asked.

Agent Carter looked at the man. "What's your name, soldier?" she asked.

"Hodge," he answered.

"Come here, Hodge," she said—and then she punched him hard in the nose.

**"And this is Agent Carter, from the British Army."**

"*OW!*" he cried.

"Get back in line, soldier," said Colonel Phillips coldly. Then he said, "There are twelve of you. But we are only looking for one man. That man will be our first Super Soldier."

The tests began.

Outside, the men had to run through woods with heavy bags on their backs. They had to climb a high wall quickly, and then move across wet ground on their stomachs. It wasn't easy for Steve, and Hodge made it harder for him. After Steve climbed to the top of the wall, Hodge pushed him to the ground again. In every test, Steve finished last.

"Rogers is the best man," Dr. Erskine said to Colonel Phillips. They stood with Agent Carter, some meters away from the twelve soldiers.

"No!" answered Colonel Phillips. "Look at him! He's too small and too thin. He's always last."

"But he never walks away," said the doctor. "Maybe he isn't strong. But he has a big heart, and that is more important."

"I like Hodge," Colonel Phillips said. "He's big and he's fast. He's a soldier."

"No," answered Dr. Erskine. "He's a bully."

"You don't win wars with nice people," said Colonel Phillips. "You win them with *brave* people. Watch this!"

The Colonel suddenly threw a small bomb into the middle of the twelve soldiers. Eleven soldiers ran for their lives. The twelfth soldier shouted, "Everybody down!" He ran to the bomb and fell on it. That soldier was Steve.

Everybody waited ... but nothing happened. Steve carefully stood up. He looked at Colonel Phillips.

"Is this a test?" he asked.

Dr. Erskine and Peggy Carter smiled. Yes, it was a test.

"O.K., O.K.," said Colonel Phillips. "The S.S.R. has its first Super Soldier. But I think he's too thin ..."

That evening, Dr. Erskine visited Steve and told him more about the plan.

"I have a serum, and it will make you a Super Soldier," he said. "You will run fast and hit hard. You will also think quickly. You will be a better soldier in every way."

"Tell me about this serum," Steve said.

"Before I came to the United States in 1937," began Dr. Erskine, "I worked in Germany. I am a scientist and I had many ideas. One idea was the Super Soldier Serum. The Nazis could never make this serum—I knew that. But, then, Johann Schmidt learned about it. Schmidt is also a scientist—a very smart and dangerous scientist."

"Is he a Nazi?" asked Steve.

"Hitler thinks that Schmidt is a Nazi, yes," Dr. Erskine told him. "But Schmidt has bigger plans. He really works for Hydra. Hydra is a bigger and older organization than the Nazis. The people of Hydra think that, somewhere, there is a great power. They call it the Tesseract. It's not from our world. Schmidt is always looking for it. I hope that he never finds it!"

"What did he want from you?" said Steve.

"He wanted my serum. He took some from me, and he used it. He was a dangerous man; now he is a *very* dangerous man, and very strong, too. I ran from Germany and brought the serum here to the United States. I am going to use it on you."

"Why me?" Steve asked.

"You are a weak man. I can change that. With the serum, you will be a very *strong* man," said Dr. Erskine. "But there is something more important. You are a good man, Steve. With the serum, you will be a *great* man."

# Into the Machine

Early the next morning, Agent Peggy Carter drove Steve to Brooklyn.

"I know these streets," said Steve. "I was in a fight in that back street ... and that street ... and behind that movie theater."

"Did you sometimes win?" asked Peggy.

"No," said Steve, "never."

"Why didn't you run away?"

"When you run, they come after you," Steve said. "Bullies never stop."

Peggy smiled. *We have the right man for the super serum*, she thought.

The car stopped outside a small, dark store, and Steve followed Peggy inside. An old woman worked there.

"The weather is wonderful this morning," Peggy said to the woman.

"Yes, it is."

"But I always carry a raincoat."

The woman smiled at Peggy's answer and opened a door at the back of the room. Peggy and Steve went down some dark stairs.

They came into a large room. It was full of strange machines. Dr. Erskine was there, with a team of scientists in white coats. There were also some film makers with a movie camera.

Inside the large room, there was a smaller room with glass walls. It was above the machines, and some men sat there. They looked important.

"That's Senator Brandt," Peggy said quietly to Steve. "The man with the gray hair at the front, next to Colonel Phillips. Brandt likes Dr. Erskine's Super Soldier plan. He got the money for all this."

"And who's that man behind him? With the black hair and glasses?" asked Steve. "He's looking at me really hard, and he doesn't look friendly."

"I'll ask somebody," said Peggy. "And behind us, that's Howard Stark."

A man at a machine with levers turned around and smiled at Peggy.

"I know him," Steve said. "He was at the show last week with the 'car of the future'! But he's not an army man."

"Mr. Stark helps with all Dr. Erskine's work in the S.S.R.," Peggy told him.

"So you know him?" Steve asked.

Before Peggy could answer, Dr. Erskine took Steve to the large machine. It was the size of a man.

"Can you climb in here, Steve?" Dr. Erskine asked, with a smile. Steve got inside. "Are you ready?"

"Yes, Doctor," answered Steve. *Was* he ready? He didn't know.

Dr. Erskine closed the machine. Everybody could see Steve's face through a small window. They could hear his heart.

"Mr. Stark?" he called. "Are *you* ready?"

"We're ready," called Stark.

Peggy went into the glass box, and Dr. Erskine spoke to everybody. "Today," he said, "we can think about the end of the war. The end of *all* wars." He showed them seven tall, thin glass bottles. "This is my serum.

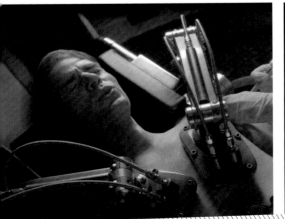

We are giving it to Private Steve Rogers of the U.S. Army. Private Rogers will be the world's first Super Soldier!"

Dr. Erskine turned to his team. "Let's begin!" he said.

Suddenly, the blue serum shot into Steve's arms and legs. *BANG! BANG! BANG!* went Steve's heart inside him. His eyes opened wide.

"Now, Mr. Stark!" called Dr. Erskine.

Stark pushed a lever. The machine, with Steve inside it, began to move. There was a very loud, high noise. Stark pushed the lever again.

"Forty … sixty …," called Stark. Steve closed his eyes. The noise was louder and higher now. People put their hands over their ears.

Stark looked at Dr. Erskine. "I'll turn it off," he shouted.

"No!" said Dr. Erskine.

"Eighty … eighty-five …"

Steve cried out.

"O.K.!" called Dr. Erskine. "Turn it off."

"No!" shouted Steve from inside the machine. "I can do this!"

Dr. Erskine looked at Howard Stark. "Go!" he said.

Stark pushed the lever one more time. "One hundred!" he cried.

Nobody spoke and nobody moved. Carefully, Dr. Erskine opened the machine. Orange and white light jumped out of the machine, and there was smoke everywhere. Then, through the smoke, Steve came out. It wasn't the old Steve. This new Steve was tall and strong.

"*OOH!*" everybody shouted.

Peggy ran to Steve. "How do you feel?" she asked.

Dr. Erskine took Steve to the large machine. It was the size of a man.

"Taller!" said Steve.

She gave him a new shirt in his new size.

The people in the glass box came out. "Great job, Erskine," said Senator Brandt.

But one man didn't smile. The man with the black hair and glasses quietly went to the bottles of serum. The serum from six of the bottles was inside Steve now. But the seventh bottle was full.

Suddenly, Dr. Erskine saw him. "You!" he shouted.

The man took the serum and turned around.

"That man's name is Kruger!" cried Dr. Erskine. "He's a Hydra agent! Stop him!"

**The man took the serum and turned around.**

# Super Soldier

It was too late.

Before people could move, Kruger threw a bomb into the center of the room.

*BANG!* It hit the large machine, and the room was suddenly full of smoke and fire.

"Stop him!" cried Dr. Erskine again. Kruger was at the door, but he turned back. He took out his gun and shot Dr. Erskine. Then, he ran.

Steve felt very strange with the serum inside him. He felt strong and weak at the same time. But when he heard the gun, he ran to Dr. Erskine.

"You can't help me, Steve," said Dr. Erskine. "You have to stop them ..."

There were no more words. He put his hand on Steve's heart, and then he died. Steve understood. He had to fight with his head *and* his heart.

He couldn't see Kruger. He ran up the stairs and into the store.

*WOW!* he thought. *I'm fast!*

But he was too late for the old woman. She was dead.

Steve ran outside. On the street, Kruger pulled a driver out of a yellow taxi. He jumped in and drove away.

"You're not getting away," Steve shouted. He ran after the taxi. He ran as quickly as his new legs could carry him. And that was fast—super fast! He was faster than the taxi and he jumped on top of it. Inside the taxi, Kruger smiled and shot above his head. He drove through the back streets to the river.

But, suddenly, a truck was in his way and he couldn't get around it. The taxi drove into the truck, and hit a wall. Steve fell onto the street. Kruger climbed out, with his gun in his hand. He shot at Steve. Steve saw the door of the taxi and used it for a shield.

Some people were next to the river. Kruger ran through them and took a young boy. He put his gun to the boy's head. Steve stopped and put his hands up. Kruger took something out of his jacket. *BEEP! BEEP!* it went. A submarine came up from under the water, next to him. Kruger threw the boy into the water and then jumped in.

*I have to save the boy,* thought Steve, *but I have to stop Kruger.*

"Go after him!" shouted the boy. "I can swim!"

"Great!" Steve shouted to him.

The new Steve could swim as fast as a fish.

Kruger's submarine moved fast under the water, but Steve quickly caught it. Kruger looked through the glass when Steve swam next to him. Steve punched the glass, and water started to run in. Steve pulled Kruger out through the window and then out of the water. He threw him to the ground.

Kruger wanted to kill Steve, and he pulled out a knife. By accident, he pulled out the bottle of serum, too. It flew out and broke on the ground.

"Who are you?" shouted Steve.

"I am the first of many men," Kruger said. "When you cut off the head of a hydra*, it gets two new heads." He put something in his mouth and broke it with his teeth. "For Hydra!" he shouted, and then he died.

The next day, everybody was at the S.S.R. Colonel Phillips was very angry.

"One small bomb, and we lost all of Dr. Erskine's work?" he shouted.

"Yes, sir," said Peggy Carter. "But they didn't get the serum, thanks to Private Rogers."

"Private Rogers!" He laughed angrily, and looked at Steve. "I asked for an army and I got *you*. *You* are *not* an army!"

Senator Brandt wasn't angry. He was happy.

"Look at this!" he cried, with the morning newspaper in his hand. There was a photo of Steve. "Yesterday, we saw our Super Soldier at work. And, more importantly, the country saw him! Now everybody wants to meet him!" He turned to Steve. "Son, I have a very important job for you."

"Yes, sir!" said Steve.

"Are you ready for important war work?"

"Yes, sir!"

"Good ... *Captain* Rogers!" said Senator Brandt.

* hydra: a large animal with many heads in old Greek stories. It lives in water. When somebody cuts off one of its heads, two new heads come in its place.

Kruger's submarine moved fast under the water, but Steve quickly caught it.

# "Where's Bucky?"

At the Nazi base in the mountains, Johann Schmidt had three important visitors.

"The Führer* gave you this base," one of them said. "Now he is waiting for your new guns and bombs. Where are they?"

"And you went to Norway, but you did not tell us!" said the second man. "The Führer is not happy with you."

"You want to see our work," Schmidt smiled. "Then we will show you! Dr. Zola, please!"

Dr. Zola started the machines. The third visitor walked to a map. It showed a Hydra bomb next to many cities around the world. One of those cities was Berlin, the center of Nazi power.

"Berlin is on this map!" he shouted.

Schmidt turned to his visitors.

"Hydra has more power than you can understand," he said slowly.

The other two visitors smiled at these words.

"Thank you, Herr** Schmidt," said the first man. "You really *are* dangerous. We can see that now. We are closing this base. Today!"

Schmidt turned a big gun to the men. They moved back.

* the Führer: a German name for Adolf Hitler, the head of the Nazis and of his country
** Herr: the German word for *Mr*.

"You are coming with us—to the Führer!" the first man shouted. He spoke angrily, but he was afraid.

*BANG!* Blue light shot out of the gun.

"Help!" shouted the other men. But they couldn't get away. The Tesseract's blue power killed them, too.

Dr. Zola moved to the door.

"Doctor!" said Schmidt. "Hydra is bigger than the Nazis. Nobody can stop us now!" He put his arm up. "For Hydra!" he shouted. Then, he waited.

Slowly, Dr. Zola put his arm up, too. "For Hydra," he said quietly.

Steve stood in a theater. He felt sick.

*I can't do this,* he thought. Steve wasn't afraid of fighting. But now he had to stand in front of the American people in theaters across the country. This was Senator Brandt's idea of an "important" job—and Steve was afraid.

It was show time. The music began. A line of girls danced and sang. "He's the man with a plan," went the song. "He's Captain America!"

"It's you now!" a man behind Steve said. Steve didn't move.

The man pushed him out in front of the theater lights. "Say your lines," the man said in his ear.

But Steve wasn't happy. He wore a mask and he carried a cheap red, white, and blue shield.

"Hi ... er ... everybody," he said. "Who's going to punch the Nazis in the face?"

"Captain America!" the children shouted happily.

After the show, their parents gave a lot of money for the war.

*Maybe this won't be too difficult,* thought Steve.

For the next six months, Steve took his Captain America show to theaters in Milwaukee and San Francisco, in Buffalo and St. Louis. In Chicago they made a film of his show, and after that his face was in movie theaters everywhere.

And then they sent him to Europe.

Senator Brandt had a new job for Steve.

"You have to sell the war to the soldiers now," he said. "They'll love you!"

Steve flew to a U.S. Army base in Italy. He wasn't in the theater now. He was in the war. Steve put on his Captain America clothes. The girls started the show, and Steve waited. Then he came out.

"Who's going to punch Adolf Hitler in the face?" he shouted.

Nobody answered. The soldiers looked at Steve and he looked at them. They were tired and hungry, and they didn't smile.

"Bring back the girls," one soldier called.

Other soldiers threw things at Steve, and he had to put up his shield. They hated Captain America.

After the show, Steve sat with his head in his hands. *Those men are fighting this war, not me,* he thought. *I'm a Super Soldier, but what do I do? I sing to them.*

"Hi, Steve."

Steve looked up. Oh, no! It was Peggy Carter!

"People say that you're famous at home," she said.

"I hope you didn't see the show," he said. "It was Senator Brandt's idea. I never wanted this life. But let's not talk about me. What are *you* doing here?"

**The soldiers looked at Steve and he looked at them. They were tired and hungry, and they didn't smile.**

"Schmidt is near here, in Austria," she said. "He's doing tests on a new Hydra bomb. We sent two hundred men to his base, but only fifty came back. Those soldiers at your show—they got back to our base. But we think that the other soldiers in the 107th Infantry are dead."

"The 107th?" repeated Steve.

"Yes, why?" Peggy asked.

"Who sent them to Schmidt's base?"

"The S.S.R.," answered Peggy. "Colonel Phillips is here."

Colonel Phillips had the names of the 107th Infantry in his hand. He had to write to their families.

"It's Captain America," said the Colonel when Steve arrived. "The man with the plan!"

"Did Sergeant Barnes come back with the 107th, sir?" asked Steve. "Please tell me—is he O.K.?"

"I'm sorry, son," said Colonel Phillips. "I remember the name. He didn't come back."

Steve saw a map on Colonel Phillips's desk. It showed the Hydra base.

"Our men are there," said Steve. "Maybe they aren't all dead. You're going to look for them, right?"

"No," said Colonel Phillips. "They're thirty kilometers behind the Nazi line, and there are too many guns. We can't lose more men. Now, I think that you have a show in ten minutes. Go!"

"Yes, sir, I have to be somewhere," said Steve. He didn't mean his show.

Outside, Peggy stopped Steve.

"What's your plan? Are you going to walk there?"

"Maybe."

"You heard the Colonel. Your friend is dead."

"This Captain America story isn't me," said Steve. "You know that. I have to go. Say yes, Agent Carter!"

Peggy thought for a minute.

"I can do more than that."

# Red Skull

Howard Stark flew his airplane over the mountains. Behind him sat Peggy Carter and Steve. Peggy had a map.

"The Hydra base is here," she said, "in Krossberg. We'll take you as near as we can."

"After Krossberg, Agent Carter," Stark said from the front of the plane, "would you like to have dinner with me in Lucerne?"

Steve looked at Peggy. He wasn't happy.

"Nobody can fly a plane better than Howard," said Peggy. "And he's brave."

"So you two ..." asked Steve. "Are you ...?"

But he didn't finish his question. Guns shot at them from the ground. Stark turned the plane to the left.

"We're near the Hydra base," he shouted.

Steve opened the door. More guns shot at them, and Howard turned to the right this time.

"After I jump," Steve said to Peggy, "get away from here!"

He jumped, and now the guns shot at *him*.

*THUD!* After some minutes, he hit the ground, and then the guns stopped.

*Good!* thought Steve. *They think I'm dead. Now, let's save some soldiers.*

Through the trees, Steve could see the Hydra base. Big lights shone down on a high wall around it.

He had to make a plan. Then, three army trucks arrived at the base and stopped. They were all open at the back. The driver in the first truck spoke to a Hydra soldier. Steve jumped into the back of the third truck. There were two soldiers inside. *POW! POW!* Steve punched them and pushed them out. The drivers started the trucks and drove into the base. He was inside!

Steve jumped out of the truck and ran to a dark doorway. He looked around. He saw a line of soldiers—American soldiers. Two Hydra soldiers pushed them through a door. Steve followed. Inside, he saw about two hundred soldiers. They weren't all Americans—there were French, Irish, and British soldiers, too. He had to get them out.

A Hydra soldier stood on some stairs above the men. Steve climbed up and punched him hard. *CRASH!* The Hydra soldier fell to the ground.

One of the American soldiers saw Steve in his red, white, and blue Captain America clothes with his cheap shield.

"Who are you?" the man asked.

"Captain America," Steve answered.

"Who?"

Steve opened the doors, and the men came out. He couldn't see Bucky.

"Are there any other men?" he asked.

"Do you see that door?" one soldier said. "One of our men is through there."

Steve ran into a very big room. He hit two Hydra soldiers with his shield, and kicked two more. The room was full of bombs of all sizes. Some were in boxes. A blue light came from the bombs. He took a small bomb and put it in his jacket.

At the end of the room, he saw offices. *Who's in there?* he thought.

There were cameras everywhere in the building, and from behind one of the doors, Schmidt and Dr. Zola could watch everything.

"Hm," said Schmidt. "One Super Soldier is very powerful!"

*BANG! BANG!* Guns! The head of Hydra looked through a different camera. "The Americans are getting out! We have to leave, too."

"Don't you think that our men ...?" Dr. Zola began.

"No, Doctor. Look! Our men are losing the fight," said Schmidt. He pushed a lever and a clock started. He carefully put the Tesseract in its box and took it with him. "We have seven minutes, Dr. Zola. Let's go!"

Schmidt and Dr. Zola left the room. Steve was behind the door, but they didn't see him. He went into the room and saw machines, papers, maps ... and a man on a table. Steve ran to him.

"Barnes," said the man weakly. His eyes were closed. "James. Sergeant."

"Bucky?" Steve said quietly. "It's me."

"Steve?" said Bucky.

Steve took Bucky's arm and helped him. He stood up slowly.

"You aren't dead!" said Steve.

"*You* aren't small and weak!" Bucky said. "What happened to you? Where's the boy from Brooklyn?"

"It's a long story," Steve told him.

*BOOM!* There was a shower of glass. The room was suddenly full of smoke.

"And now, we have to get out of here," Steve said.

At the door, he stopped and looked at a map on the wall. It showed every Hydra base in Europe.

*BOOM! BOOM!* More bombs!

"We heard about a Super Soldier," Bucky said. "That's you! Did it hurt?"

"Yes," said Steve.

They came to some stairs. They could go up or down. *CRASH!* A wall fell onto the stairs. Now they could only go up.

They went through a door and stopped. They were high up in a large room. Below them were machines, but they were all on fire. *BOOM!* Another bomb.

"Captain America! How exciting!" somebody said. It was Johann Schmidt, and he and Dr. Zola were in Steve's way. "I love your movies." Schmidt gave the Tesseract to Dr. Zola. Then, he spoke to Steve again. "So, Dr. Erskine gave you his serum. But people say that he died. How sad!"

Steve angrily punched Schmidt as hard as he could. The head of Hydra fell. He stood up and smiled before he punched Steve.

**Under the mask, he had no face—only a skull.**

"*OUF!*" said Steve. Schmidt was as strong as he was. Then, Steve jumped into him feet first.

Dr. Zola ran to a door and quickly opened it. He called to Schmidt.

Schmidt stood up. His face looked very strange. His left eye was higher than his right eye! Suddenly, with an ugly smile, Schmidt put his hand on his face and pulled. It came off in his hand! His face was a mask! Under the mask, he had no face—only a skull. Now he was Red Skull, and he laughed crazily. He took the Tesseract from Dr. Zola. Then, he turned and walked away. The door closed behind him.

*BOOM!* The floor fell away. Steve and Bucky couldn't follow them. They couldn't get out.

Steve looked around him. He could see a door across the room, but he couldn't get to it. Steve took Bucky in his arms and threw him across to the door.

*BOOM! BOOM!*

Now the room was full of fire.

"Get out!" Steve shouted. "Go!"

"Not without you," Bucky shouted to him.

There was only one way out. Steve had to jump.

# 7

## *The Man with a Plan*

"*I'm very sorry ... but Captain Steve Rogers is dead ...,*" Colonel Phillips wrote. He looked up when Agent Carter came in. "I'm writing to Senator Brandt," he said.

Peggy looked tired and sad. But Colonel Phillips didn't feel sorry for her. He was angry with her.

"I can't say anything to Stark," he said to Peggy. "He's rich, and he makes our guns. But *you* ...!"

"I'm leaving in the morning," answered Peggy. "I'm not sorry, Colonel. We did the right thing."

"Captain America is dead because you helped him," Colonel Phillips said. "A lot of other men are dead, too. And why? Because you liked Captain America's face."

"No, sir," answered Peggy. "It wasn't that—"

Suddenly, there was a lot of noise outside. Soldiers ran past the window. Some shouted. Colonel Phillips and Peggy went outside.

There, on the road into the base, was Captain America. Next to him was Bucky. Behind them, there were more than two hundred soldiers. Most of them walked. Some of them drove Hydra trucks. They were tired and dirty, but they weren't dead. They were free!

"Some of these men have to see a doctor, sir," Steve told Colonel Phillips. "And I want to say sorry."

Colonel Phillips looked at Steve. Steve's eyes shone. He was a different man.

"Good work, Captain Rogers," the Colonel said, and he walked away.

And there was Peggy. Steve's heart jumped when he saw her.

She looked into his eyes. "You're late," she said.

The next week, everybody was at the S.S.R.'s London office. Peggy had a newspaper. *The Man with a Plan*—it said—*Captain America Saves Two Hundred Men!* But Steve wasn't interested in newspapers. He was only interested in their *next* plan.

There was a map of Europe on the table. Steve remembered the map on the wall of Red Skull's office, and put an *X* on it for each Hydra base. The small bomb with Red Skull's blue power was on the table.

"What's this, Stark?" asked Colonel Phillips.

"It has more power than our bombs," Stark answered. "I know this isn't possible ... but ... I don't think it's from our world." He didn't look happy. "We can't win this war."

Colonel Phillips looked at the map. "Are these all their bases?" he asked.

"There's one more," said Steve. "And most of the bombs are there. It wasn't on the map in Red Skull's office, but Red Skull and Zola talked about it in front of Sergeant Barnes."

"That will be the most important base," Peggy said. "We have to find it."

"Agent Carter," said Colonel Phillips, "that's your job. Captain Rogers, find a team of men and visit every base on this map. Can you do that?"

"Yes, sir!" Steve smiled.

That evening, Steve found his team in a bar in the center of town. There was Bucky, of course, and five other men, all from different countries and all from the Hydra base in Krossberg. Now, they were all Steve's friends. Steve told them the plan.

"We only got out of a Hydra base yesterday," they laughed. "And you want us to go into *more* Hydra bases! No problem, Captain!"

There was music in the bar. The men asked some girls for a dance.

Steve bought Bucky a drink. "So you're following Captain America?" Steve asked.

"No," Bucky answered. "I'm following the boy from the back streets of Brooklyn. Remember him? He never walked away from a fight, and he had a big heart. I'm following *him*."

Then, Peggy Carter walked in. She usually wore her brown army clothes. This evening, she looked beautiful in a red dress.

"Good evening, Agent Carter," Steve said.

"Good evening, Captain Rogers," said Peggy. "Mr. Stark wants you in his office tomorrow morning. Eight o'clock."

She looked at Steve's men. "Is this your team?" she asked. "Do they always drink before they fight a war? And dance?"

"Don't you like music?" Bucky asked.

"I *love* music," answered Peggy. She spoke to Bucky, but she looked at Steve. "I'll go dancing when this ends."

Steve felt good. He was a soldier. His best friend was with him. He had a great team. And maybe he had a future with Peggy. Yes, he felt *really* good.

**This evening, she looked beautiful in a red dress.**

# "I'll Never See Him Again."

Then, Steve's hopes for the future changed again.

He arrived early at Howard Stark's office.

"He'll be here in a minute," said a young woman behind a desk.

Steve sat down and waited.

"For all the women of America ...," the young woman said, "I want to thank you." She stood up and put her arms around him.

"Captain Rogers!" It was Peggy. "We're ready for you now! Or are you too busy?"

She turned and walked angrily away.

Steve ran after her. "Agent Carter!" he called. "Wait! Peggy!"

"Save your words," she answered. "You're the same as the other soldiers."

"And you and Stark?" he asked.

Peggy stopped. "Stark and me?" she repeated, and laughed. "You have no idea about women!"

Stark heard their conversation and smiled. They followed him through a door into a room full of busy scientists.

"This way," said Stark. On a table, there were some new clothes for Steve. Steve felt them with his fingers.

"What *is* this?" he asked.

"Everybody will wear this in the future," Stark said, with a laugh. "But now, only you. It will save you from knives and guns. But maybe not from Hydra's blue bombs."

On another table, there was a line of shields!

"You like your shield, right?" Stark smiled. "These are the *best*."

Steve looked at them all, and then went to a round shield. It was light and beautiful.

"Tell me about *this* shield," he said.

"It's vibranium*. Very strong and very light. No gun can shoot through that."

Steve loved it. He showed it to Peggy.

"What do you think?" he asked.

She took out her gun and shot at Steve four times. She hit the shield four times, and it didn't break.

"Yes, I think it works," she said coldly.

She turned and walked away.

For the next six months, Captain America and his team went across Europe. They found the Hydra bases in France, Poland, Czechoslovakia, and Greece. After each visit, Peggy put a line through the Hydra *X* on the map. She wrote *S.S.R.* in its place.

"This has to stop!" Red Skull shouted at Dr. Zola, on the phone from his base in the mountains. "It has to stop *now!*"

Then, his ugly face smiled an ugly smile. He had an idea. It was a very good idea.

* vibranium: Nothing in the Marvel Universe is stronger than vibranium. You can only find it in Wakanda, an African country.

Steve, Bucky, and the team stood on a mountain in the Alps*. It was early in the morning, and the wind was very cold.

"Something's not right, Bucky," said Steve. "We're listening to their radio, but it's too easy."

"Maybe," Bucky answered. "But maybe we can finish Hydra today. We have to try."

The team's radio man, Jones, called up to Steve. "The Hydra base is talking to the train, Captain. Dr. Zola is on the train with the bombs. The Hydra base says that they have to go faster."

Then, they heard the sound of a train.

"We have to get this right first time, men," Steve shouted. "Let's do this!"

The train came nearer. It was below them. Now!

*WHOOSH!* Steve, Bucky, and Jones pushed away from the mountain.

*THUD!* They hit the top of the train. Jones was at the front. He had to stop the train.

Steve and Bucky wanted Dr. Zola and the bombs. The train had six cars. They climbed into the back car. There was nothing in it. That was strange. They climbed into the next car. Again, there was nothing in it. The third car was very dark. And it was very quiet. It was *too* quiet.

*WHAM!* Behind Steve, a door closed between him and Bucky. The lights came on. Steve now saw a very large Hydra soldier. He was more than two meters tall, with big guns in place of arms. This was Red Skull's plan. Kill Steve. Kill the U.S. Army's only Super Soldier. Then, nobody could stop Hydra!

* the Alps: the highest mountains in Europe. They are in Germany, Austria, France, Switzerland, Italy, Slovenia, Liechtenstein, and Monaco.

Steve shot the soldier with his gun, but nothing happened. The Hydra soldier then shot Steve from one of his "arms."

*POW!* Blue power threw Steve off his feet. He hit the wall of the train and fell to the floor.

But Steve was a Super Soldier. He jumped up and hit the soldier with his vibranium shield. Steve ran back to the door and saw Bucky through the window. There was a Hydra soldier in his car, too. Bucky didn't have his gun now. Steve opened the car door and threw his gun to Bucky. Then he jumped in. Bucky shot the soldier.

"I was O.K.," Bucky smiled. "You didn't have to help me!"

"I know," Steve said.

The Hydra soldier was on his feet again. Blue power shot through one wall of the train. They could see the mountains. The soldier shot at them again. Bucky fell back, almost out of the train car. Steve shot at the soldier and killed him. He put his hand out to Bucky.

"Take my hand, Bucky!" he shouted over the wind.

But the train turned suddenly to the left, and Bucky fell down to the cold ice below.

"*NO!*" cried Steve. Bucky was his oldest friend—his *best* friend. *He's dead*, thought Steve. *I'll never see him again*.

Steve climbed sadly back inside the car. He saw Jones in the next car. Jones pushed Dr. Zola in front of him with his gun. They had Hydra's top scientist.

"Good job," Colonel Phillips said on the radio.

It didn't feel that way to Steve.

"Something's not right, Bucky," said Steve. "We're listening to their radio, but it's too easy."

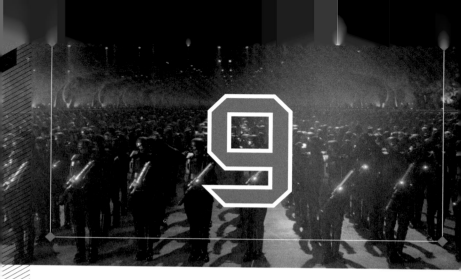

# 9

# *Under the Mountain*

"I don't eat meat," Dr. Zola told Colonel Phillips.

The scientist and the soldier sat in a small room at the London base of the S.S.R. There was a plate of meat and vegetables between them.

"*I'll* eat it," said Colonel Phillips. "This is war time. You have to eat when you can."

The Colonel asked Dr. Zola many questions. Dr. Zola didn't answer any of them.

"I'll show you something," the Colonel said.

It was a note from London to Washington D.C. It said: *This morning, Dr. Zola told us everything about Red Skull and his plans. We are now sending Dr. Zola to Switzerland.*

"Shall I send this?" the Colonel asked. "Your boss will read it, of course. And he'll find you and kill you. It's you or him, Doctor."

Dr. Zola thought about this. He had to tell them everything.

"What are Red Skull's plans?" Colonel Phillips asked.

"Red Skull will never stop," said Dr. Zola. "He wants the world."

"You know that's crazy, right?"

"Of course. But he can do it. He has the power. He has the Tesseract."

"Where will he send his bombs?" asked Colonel Phillips.

"Everywhere," Dr. Zola answered. He had a strange smile on his face. "Listen. I will tell you about his power ..."

Phillips called the S.S.R. team into his office and told them about Red Skull's plans.

"He's going to start with the United States," the Colonel said. "He'll fly across the Atlantic, and in one hour, that will be the end of New York City, Boston, and Washington D.C."

"How much time have we got?" Steve asked.

"Twenty-four hours," answered Colonel Phillips.

"And where is Red Skull now?"

"At his base in the Alps, here," said Colonel Phillips. He put his finger on the map.

"This won't be easy," Steve said. "But we can do it. We *have* to do it."

Everybody flew to the Alps.

Then, Steve drove through the woods to the base. He thought about Red Skull. *Only two of us in the world have Dr. Erskine's serum inside us—Red Skull and me. Today, we will fight. Who is stronger—him or me?*

After some kilometers, he saw the wall of the Hydra base in front of him. Soldiers stood on the wall with guns and waited for him. But that was fine. That was the plan.

The Hydra soldiers brought Captain America to Red Skull. One wall of his office was all glass. On another wall, there was a large picture of Red Skull.

"You are strong, Captain, but you are not as strong as me," he said.

"You're right," said Steve. "I'm only a boy from Brooklyn. But I don't like bullies."

*POW!* Red Skull hit Steve, and he went down. Steve kicked Red Skull, but not very hard. Red Skull caught his foot and threw him into a wall.

Steve stood up. "I can do this all day!" he said.

"I think you can," said Red Skull. "But I don't *have* all day." He pulled out a gun.

Steve smiled. Red Skull had his back to the window. He didn't see Steve's team.

*CRASH!* Glass flew everywhere. And Steve flew feet first into Red Skull.

Red Skull shouted angrily. He got up and took the box with the Tesseract. He ran out of the room. More Hydra soldiers came in and shot at Steve and his men.

*BLAM!* The Hydra soldiers fell to the ground. Colonel Phillips was behind them, with a large gun.

Steve found his shield and followed Red Skull.

When Red Skull saw Steve behind him, he shot at him. Blue power from the gun hit Steve's vibranium shield. He didn't feel it. *This shield is really great!* Steve thought.

Now he couldn't see Red Skull, but he heard noises from some big doors. He had to get there before they closed. He threw his shield. *THUNK!* The heavy doors stopped, with the shield between them.

Then, there was a large Hydra soldier between him and the doors. The soldier had a very big gun. Steve had no gun and no shield. He had no more ideas.

*BLAM!* Somebody shot the Hydra soldier from behind him.

Out of the smoke came Agent Carter!

"You're late!" he said, and smiled at her. Peggy smiled at him.

When Steve was through the doors, he pulled out his shield. *BANG!* The doors closed behind him. And then, he stopped, eyes wide. In front of him were six airplanes. They were four times as big as a U.S. Army plane. *They're going to carry the blue bombs*, Steve thought. *They're going to take them to the United States.*

One of the planes started to move. Steve saw its name: the *Valkyrie*. And through its window, he saw Red Skull. The ugly face turned and laughed. "You can't stop me now!"

The big doors at the other end of the room opened to the sky.

The plane moved fast. Captain America ran after it. He was fast, but not as fast as a plane. He couldn't catch it. But then, a car came past him. It was Red Skull's car, but Colonel Phillips and Peggy were in it. Steve jumped in, and Colonel Phillips drove the car under the *Valkyrie*. Captain America stood up.

"Wait!" shouted Peggy, and put her arms around him. For a very short time, Steve forgot about Red Skull and Hydra. And for the first time in his life, Steve Rogers got the girl. But then, he had to go.

"You can do it, Captain America!" shouted Colonel Phillips.

Steve jumped up into the *Valkyrie*, and it left the ground.

Steve had to stop this plane with its blue bombs before it got across the ocean. One man stood in his way—Red Skull. Steve was tired. His arms and legs hurt. But he had to be brave. He had to do this for his country, for Peggy, and for Bucky.

*POW!* Red Skull hit Steve, and he went down.

# 10

## *Fight to the End*

Steve's job was suddenly more difficult. Inside the *Valkyrie,* there were eight fighter planes. Next to each plane, there was a Hydra soldier. Each soldier had a blue gun. And they all looked at Steve.

They couldn't use their guns inside the plane, so Steve used his feet and his shield. He kicked the first two soldiers to the floor. He threw the next two into a wall. He hit one soldier in the face with his shield. But then, the sixth soldier punched Steve from behind. He fell back onto one of the fighter planes. A soldier was inside and started the plane. It shot out of the back of the *Valkyrie*, into the open sky.

Steve climbed across the top of the plane to its window. The soldier turned the plane quickly three times, but he couldn't lose Steve. Steve's super strong arms saved him.

He moved nearer to the window and punched through the glass. He pulled the soldier out of the window and climbed in. The plane started to fall to the ground. Steve quickly turned it around. The *Valkyrie* was some kilometers away now, and Steve flew as fast as he could. He brought the fighter plane into the *Valkyrie* again and stopped it. There were two more Hydra soldiers, but he was too strong for them. Steve jumped out of the fighter plane and threw his shield at them.

Now the most important job began.

Steve went to the front of the *Valkyrie*. Where was Red Skull? Steve heard something. He knew that sound, and he quickly put up his shield. It stopped the blue power from Red Skull's gun.

Red Skull shot again, but this time he hit the front windows of the plane. The glass broke and—*WHOOSH!*—the wind came in.

Steve and Red Skull fought hard. In the middle of the fight, Steve fell onto a lever, and suddenly, the *Valkyrie* flew down fast. Red Skull pulled the lever back, and the plane was on its way to New York City again, to Steve's home town.

Red Skull took out a smaller gun. It shone blue. He shot at Steve, but the vibranium shield saved Captain America again.

"You know that I'm going to win. Why don't you stop fighting?" Red Skull shouted.

"Never!" Steve shouted.

"Don't fight me, Captain Rogers!" shouted Red Skull. "Fight *with* me. Hydra is the future."

"That's not *my* future," Steve said. He threw his shield as hard as he could. It hit Red Skull first, and then the machine with the Tesseract. *CRACK! CRACK!* Blue light jumped around the plane.

Steve could see the power of the Tesseract. Then, something very strange happened. The Tesseract opened a window into space. Steve looked out with wide eyes.

"What did you do?" shouted Red Skull. He took the Tesseract in his hand but it was more powerful than him.

"*No!*" he cried. The blue light first ate his hand, and then his arms and legs. And then, he wasn't there.

The blue light went out. The Tesseract fell to the floor. It ate through the floor of the plane and fell down to the cold ocean below.

The plane was over the Arctic now. Steve pulled and pushed every lever, but nothing worked. He found the plane's radio and called the S.S.R.

"Hello?" he said. "Hello? This is Captain Rogers. Is anybody there? Can you hear me?"

At Schmidt's base, the S.S.R. team suddenly heard Captain America.

Peggy answered. "Steve? Is that you? Are you all right?"

"I'm fine," he said. "Red Skull's dead."

"And the plane?" asked Peggy.

"That's more difficult," Steve answered.

"Where are you?" Peggy asked. "We have bases in Greenland and Canada … You can bring the plane down in one of them."

"Peggy, I can't move the plane right or left. It's going to New York City and I can't change it. I can only do one thing. I can go down. I have to put it in the water."

"Steve!" cried Peggy. "We have time. Don't do it!"

Steve saw ice and water below him. He had about one minute before he was over cities and towns. He pushed on the lever as hard as he could. The *Valkyrie*'s nose went down, and it flew fast. The ice and water came nearer.

"Peggy," he said.

"I'm here," she said.

"I can't go dancing tonight."

"All right," Peggy answered. "Next Saturday, then. At the Stork Club. Eight o'clock. Don't be late."

"I can't dance. You know that, right?"

"I'll teach you," she said. "But be there."

*BUZZZZ …*

# "Where Am I?"

Steve woke up in a strange room. He sat up, and he felt fine. He felt great. The window was open and outside the sun shone.

Was he in a hospital? He looked at his clothes. He wore an S.S.R. T-shirt and army pants.

What did he remember? He was in the *Valkyrie* and Peggy asked him to the Stork Club on Saturday night. Then, nothing.

The radio was on in the room. It was a baseball game—it was Steve's home team—but something wasn't right.

A woman came into the room. "Good morning," she said.

"Where am I?" Steve asked.

"You're in New York City," she said. He looked at her and thought of Peggy. He had to be at the Stork Club, at eight o'clock. What day was it? Was it Saturday?

He listened to the game again.

"Something's wrong," he said. "This is an *old* game, from May 1941. I was there! Where am I really?"

"I don't understand," said the woman.

Steve stood up.

"Captain Rogers—" she began.

He quickly walked around her and opened the door. There were soldiers outside. But they weren't from the U.S. Army and they weren't Nazis.

Steve pushed past them, out of the room. It was a small room in the center of a bigger room, and there was an open door at one end. With his super strong legs, he ran to the door. Nobody could catch him.

He was in the heart of New York City, and he knew the street. He ran into Times Square and looked around him. Everything was different. The buildings were taller. They were all glass. The clothes were … strange. And the cars were from the future. It was Howard Stark's world of tomorrow, but today.

Then, six big, black cars stopped around Steve. Soldiers in black got out. A man with no hair and one eye spoke to Steve.

"Everything's fine, Captain," he said. "I'm sorry about that little show back there. Things are different than …"

"Than what?"

"Than when you last saw the world. You were asleep for almost seventy years," the man said.

Steve couldn't speak.

"Are you going to be O.K.?" asked the man with one eye.

"Yes," Steve said slowly.

He looked around at his new world—and he thought about Peggy.

"But I'm late," he said. "I'm too late."

**He looked around at his new world—and he thought about Peggy.**

# Activities

## Chapters 1–2

### Before you read

---

**1** What do you know about Captain America? What does the picture on the front of the book tell you about him?

**2** Look at the Word List at the back of the book. Finish these sentences with the best word.

　**a** You drive a(n) … .
　**b** You fight a(n) … .
　**c** You wear a(n) … .
　**d** You carry a(n) … .
　**e** You pull a(n) … .

**3** Find these words in your dictionary, and answer the questions.

　*captain*　*colonel*　*private*　*senator*　*sergeant*

　**a** Which of these people is not a soldier?
　**b** Which is the most important of these soldiers, in the U.S. Army?

**4** Read Who's Who? and the Introduction, and answer these questions.

　**a** Who are best friends?
　**b** Who left Germany at the start of the war?
　**c** Who is the head of the S.S.R.?
　**d** Who is a British agent?
　**e** Who is a Swiss scientist?
　**f** Who is the head of Hydra?
　**g** What changes Steve Rogers into a Super Soldier?
　**h** What started in 1939?
　**i** What brought the United States into the war?

## While you read

**5** Are these sentences right (✔) or wrong (✘)?

**a** Johann Schmidt finds the Tesseract. ◯
**b** Bucky saves a big man from a fight with Steve. ◯
**c** Steve isn't interested in the army or the war in Europe. ◯
**d** Howard Stark will have to do more work on the car of the future. ◯
**e** Schmidt and Zola are using the Tesseract's power for bombs. ◯
**f** Dr. Erskine is going to give the Super Soldier Serum to Steve. ◯

## After you read

**6** What do you learn about Johann Schmidt, Steve Rogers, and Dr. Erskine in these chapters? Write two sentences about each man.

# Chapters 3-5

## Before you read

**7** How will the serum change Steve? What do you think?

## While you read

**8** Underline the best words in *italics*.

**a** Peggy *knows / doesn't know* the man with black hair and glasses behind Senator Brandt.
**b** Dr. Erskine wants to *fight more wars / end all wars* with his Super Soldier plan.
**c** The serum *works / doesn't work*.
**d** Kruger shoots Dr. Erskine; Steve *saves / can't save* him.
**e** Steve can run super fast now *and he catches / but he can't catch* Kruger in the yellow taxi.
**f** Kruger gets away from Steve in *an airplane / a submarine*.
**g** *Senator Brandt / Colonel Phillips* has a new job for Steve.

**9** Which of these happen? Write *yes* or *no*.

    **a** Johann Schmidt kills his three Nazi visitors. ....................

    **b** Dr. Zola says that he loves the Führer, not Hydra. ....................

    **c** Steve speaks to people in theaters across America. ....................

    **d** The soldiers tell Steve that his show is great. ....................

    **e** Peggy tells Steve that Bucky is dead. ....................

    **f** Steve sees the Hydra base on a map. ....................

## After you read

**10** Discuss this question. How does Steve feel about his Captain America show, in the U.S. and in Europe?

# Chapters 6-8

## Before you read

**11** Answer these questions. What do you think?

    **a** What is Steve's plan? Will Peggy help him?

    **b** The next chapter is "Red Skull." Find the word *skull* in your dictionary. Who is Red Skull?

## While you read

**12** Finish these sentences with the best words.

    **a** When they get near Krossberg, Steve has to .................................... out of the plane.

    **b** Steve gets into the base inside an army .................................... .

    **c** Schmidt says that his men are .................................... the fight.

    **d** Steve finds his best friend; Bucky isn't .................................... !

    **e** Steve sees every Hydra base on a .................................... on the wall of Schmidt's room.

    **f** Schmidt has no face under his .................................... .

**13** Who is speaking? Who are they talking to?

**a** "We can't win this war."

_____ to _____

**b** "I'm following the boy from the back streets of Brooklyn."

_____ to _____

**c** "You have no idea about women."

_____ to _____

**d** "This has to stop!"

_____ to _____

**e** "Something's not right ..."

_____ to _____

## After you read

**14** You are in Captain America's team, and you are going to a small Hydra base in the mountains in Poland. You have to close the base there. Make a plan. How will you get into the base? How will you stop the Hydra soldiers? How will you get home again?

# Chapters 9–11

## Before you read

**15** Colonel Phillips wants to know about Red Skull's plans. What will he ask Dr. Zola? Write three questions.

## While you read

**16** Answer these questions.

**a** Why doesn't Colonel Phillips send his note to the United States?
Because _____

**b** Why are Red Skull's bombs very powerful?
Because _____

**c** Why is Red Skull as strong as Captain America?
Because _____

**d** Why doesn't the large Hydra soldier kill Steve?
Because _____

**17** <u>Underline</u> the wrong word(s). Write the right word(s).

    **a** Red Skull is flying the *Valkyrie* to London.    .................................

    **b** Red Skull wants Steve to fight with the Nazis.    .................................

    **c** Steve kills Red Skull.    .................................

    **d** The Tesseract falls into the night sky.    .................................

    **e** Peggy saves Steve and the *Valkyrie*.    .................................

**18** Answer these questions.

    **a** When Steve wakes up, where is he?

    ........................................................................

    **b** What three things are different outside?

    ........................................................................

    ........................................................................

    ........................................................................

    **c** "I'm late," says Steve. Who is he thinking about?

    ........................................................................

## *After you read*

**19** Discuss these questions. What will Captain America do now? Will he stay in the army? Will he look for the Tesseract? Will he look for Peggy?

# *Writing*

**20** The *Valkyrie* goes into the ocean. Then, everybody thinks that Steve is dead. Write about his life for a newspaper. Start like this: *Captain Steve Rogers was born in the last year of World War I, and he died in the last year of World War II.*

**21** After a very long sleep, you wake up seventy years later, in the future. How is life different? How is it the same? Write ten sentences.

**22** It is two months after Steve and the *Valkyrie* fall into the ocean. Peggy writes to a friend about Steve, their fight with Red Skull, and her feelings now. Write her letter.

**23** You are Dr. Erskine. At the beginning of the book, he is looking for a soldier for his serum. Write about the job for the Lehigh base newspaper. Start like this: *Do you want to be a Super Soldier? Your country is looking for the right man. You have to be ... You can't be ...*

**24** You are a scientist in the U.S. Army. A submarine finds the Tesseract at the bottom of the ocean. People bring it to you. You don't know anything about the Tesseract. What is it? What does it do? Write your ideas about it for your boss. Find new words in your dictionary.

**25** Think about another ending to the story. Steve doesn't fall into the ocean. He flies to Canada and goes to New York City. He meets Peggy at the Stork Club on Saturday at eight o'clock. Write their conversation.

**26** What do you like about this story? What do you not like? Write about your feelings.

# *Word List*

**agent (n)** Jim Nicholson worked for the CIA, a U.S. *agency*, for years, but he was a Russian *agent* at the same time.

**army (n)** Germany had a large *army* in 1939, and was ready for war.

**base (n)** The company has one *base* in Spain and one in Argentina. A hundred people work at each *base*.

**baseball (n)** We're going to the *baseball* game on Saturday, and the Red Sox are going to win!

**bomb (n)** After the *bomb* fell on the building, there was smoke and fire everywhere.

**brave (adj)** *Brave* firefighters carried the children out of the building before it fell down.

**bully (n)** The *bullies* took the girl's phone and broke it. Then they laughed at her.

**heart (n)** A person dies when his or her *heart* stops. A person with a *big heart* is a good and kind person.

**lever (n)** He pulled one *lever* and pushed another. The machine started to work.

**mask (n)** When a person is wearing a *mask*, you cannot see his or her face.

**organization (n)** There are 193 countries in the U.N. It is a very large and important *organization*.

**power (n)** I can't drive fast. This car doesn't have much *power*. It isn't very *powerful*.

**punch (n/v)** He hurt his hand when he angrily *punched* the wall.

**save (v)** She jumped into the river and *saved* my life.

**science (n)** I want to be a doctor and I study hard in *science* classes at school. A *scientist* works in *science*.

**serum (n)** Doctors take *serum* from people or animals. It can then help other people when they are sick. It can also help in hospital tests.

**shield (n)** Carry your *shield* in front of you. Then people can't hurt you.

**show (n)** The students did a funny *show* in the school theater at the end of the year.

**soldier (n)** A *soldier* fights in an army, and often carries a gun.

**space (n)** They flew a long way from the Earth, into *space*.

**submarine (n)** The *submarine* stayed under water for months, with 120 people inside it.

**super (adj/adv)** Peter is *super* strong. He can kick a wall down with one foot.

**team (n)** The football *team* lost their first ten games; then, they won the next ten games.

**truck (n)** Each army *truck* took twenty soldiers to the next town.

**war (n)** The war ended, but in some cities the fighting didn't stop.